Formation for ministry within a learning church

The structure and funding of ordination training

A summary of the report
GS Misc 710

Church House Publishing
Church House
Great Smith Street
London SW1P 3NZ

ISBN: 978-0-7151-4354-4

GS Misc 710

Published 2003 for the Ministry Division of the Archbishops' Council by Church House Publishing

Copyright © The Archbishops' Council 2003

All rights reserved. No part of this publication may be reproduced or stored or transmitted by any means or in any form, electronic or mechanical, including photocopying, recording, or any information storage and retrieval system, without written permission which should be sought from the Copyright Administrator, The Archbishops' Council, Church House, Great Smith Street, London SWIP 3NZ.

Tel: 020 7898 1594
Fax: 020 7898 1449
Email: copyright@c-of-e.org.uk

Cover design by Visible Edge

Printed in England by Halstan & Co. Ltd, Amersham, Bucks

FORMATION FOR MINISTRY WITHIN A LEARNING CHURCH

THE STRUCTURE AND FUNDING OF ORDINATION TRAINING

Summary of the report
April 2003

> This paper summarizes the final report of the working party on the structure and funding of ordination training. It outlines the thinking behind the main proposals which have been put forward following consultation with the dioceses, our training institutions and our partners in other churches and in higher education.

1 Introduction

i) In March 2000 the Archbishops' Council of the Church of England set up a review of the structure and funding of ordination training to be chaired by Bishop John Hind. It endorsed the report in March 2003 and commended it to the General Synod for debate in July 2003. The terms of reference and membership of the working party are given in Appendix A and B. The report in full can be found on the Church of England website at www.cofe.anglican.org

ii) The report has been produced through the working party's own deliberations and through three rounds of consultation with the Archbishops' Council, the House of Bishops, dioceses, theological colleges, courses and OLM schemes, ecumenical partners and institutions of higher education. After a preliminary request for views in 2000, it circulated an interim report in February 2002 and a draft final report in November 2002. The working party is grateful to all those who have contributed to this debate and believes that its proposals now represent a broad consensus of opinion.

2 Contents of the report

The chapter headings of the full report are:

1 Introduction

2 The issues that have driven our work

3 Theological priorities for ministry

4 Lifelong learning: a better-trained clergy

5 A new framework for ministerial education

6 Reconfiguring the Church's training resources: proposals concerning training institutions

7 Financial issues

8 Encouraging and managing flexibility: some further training issues

9 List of proposals and outlook

3 The key issues

The working party has identified the following list of issues as the key ones for its work. We have reviewed the current provision for the ministerial education and formation of the clergy, in the context of the Church's total provision for ministerial training, lay training and formal lay adult education.[1] In other words, we have set the

---

[1] In the report we distinguish between adult lay education which is the responsibility of parishes, with some resourcing by the dioceses, and what we have called formal lay theological education. By the latter, which we address in this report, we mean the diocesan provision for lay theological education at a

particular learning of the clergy within the education of the whole people of God for its mission in the world. In addition we have noted the achievements of our current training establishment and reviewed current issues in initial ministerial education (IME). Against this background, we have attempted to make a contribution in the following areas:

i) outlining theological principles that underlie the Church of England's ministry;

ii) rethinking the initial ministerial education of the clergy so that it begins in a substantial way before ordination and continues in a structured and related way in the early years of ministry, as a contribution to stimulating lifelong learning;

iii) considering how to set ministerial education for the clergy within the context of a coordinated provision for adult learning and training in the Church – IME and CME (continuing ministerial education) for clergy and Readers, training for other lay ministries and formal theological education for lay discipleship;

iv) promoting a country-wide initiative for formal theological education for lay people and for a range of lay ministries, while enabling potential candidates for ordained ministry to embark on basic studies in Christian theology and issues about ministry before they enter training;

v) addressing the issue of the smallness of many of our training institutions and the lack of coordination between them with a view to making better use of the Church's current resources in training;

vi) creating a structure that has potential to be developed with our ecumenical partners in other churches;

vii) maximizing the benefits of partnership:

---

level that is, or could be, accredited, in higher education terms, at Level 1 or access levels.

a) between providers of ministerial education;

b) with UK higher education, including universities and the church colleges of higher education;

viii) making proposals for a well-structured, but appropriately flexible, framework for learning, within a continued financial discipline, for candidates for ordained ministry;

ix) establishing norms for the theological and ministerial qualification of the clergy;

x) proposing a secure place for research for the benefit of the Church alongside the education and training functions of our institutions;

xi) reviewing the Church's financial investment in training, with a view to increasing the proportion which goes into education and training as opposed to personal and family maintenance;

xii) investigating the possibility of public funding for our training institutions.

4 The proposals

Our proposals are set out here, with a short explanation of the thinking behind each of them. A much fuller version of our analysis and thinking is available in the main report which includes an essay on the theology of ministry and sections on formation and the use of residence in ministerial training.

5 Initial training and lifelong learning

Our starting point for considering the formation and training of the clergy is the goal of promoting lifelong learning. No system of initial training should aim to give all the training, formation and education required for ministry 'upfront'. Rather it should seek to give an adequate basis for the beginning of ministry and, further, set ministers on the pathway towards lifelong learning. However, as currently configured, we believe there is a 'fault line' in the organization of the ministerial education of the clergy between the pre-ordination and post-ordination phases. Theological colleges, courses and OLM schemes are responsible for the former, while training incumbents and diocesan CME officers oversee the latter. For candidates there is little or no visible connection between the two phases of training. Our proposal is to reconfigure initial training, so that it extends from entry into training, up to ordination and throughout the first curacy, in order to give a powerful impetus to setting up patterns of lifelong learning in the clergy.

Proposal 1

We recommend that initial ministerial education be reconfigured as the period from entry into training to the end of the first training post.

6 A new framework for learning

Currently, decisions about the length, mode (part-time, full-time, mixed-mode) and, therefore, the cost of the initial training of ordinands are made in the light of three main factors. These are:

i) a candidate's age (particularly whether or not a candidate is below or above 30);

ii) category of sponsorship;

iii) whether or not the candidate is a theology graduate.

This approach is codified in bishops' regulations for training. However, we believe that the regulations are no longer appropriate at several points. For example, in a Church which has relatively few candidates who are under 30, able 30-year-olds still need special permission to undertake the three years of full-time training to enable them to take a theology degree as part of their pre-ordination training. Thus we need a more flexible approach to meet the training needs of today's candidates. In the light of this, we propose a new framework for ministerial education. The key features would be:

   a) agreed phases of development in a formational journey, from entry into training up to appointment to a post of responsibility, which are marked by specified levels of achievement in ministerial education. Thus, the framework would be based around the phases of exploring vocation and undertaking preliminary studies; a pre-ordination phase of IME; a post-ordination phase from ordination to the end of the first training post; and further ministerial development in a post of responsibility or a further assistant post.

   b) a statement that would indicate the qualities and learning expected of candidates at the important thresholds (entry into training; ordination; appointment to a post of responsibility).

While we have so far only addressed the needs of ordinands and of the newly ordained, this framework of learning could easily be developed in order to integrate other types of learning. Thus, a broader framework could be developed to include Readers, other lay ministers and other forms of formal lay education, as well as later CME for Readers and clergy. Such a framework would allow credit to be given to those who have undergone training in one context who proceed to other forms of training. For example, someone who has trained as a Reader could both be given credit for their previous study and have a clear statement of their further goals in training and formation.

Proposal 2

We recommend that the current bishops' regulations for training be replaced by a framework for ministerial education, based on:

i)   **agreed phases of development in a formational journey, and**

iii) statements indicating the qualities and learning expected of candidates at key points in that journey.

7 Theological education in the wider Church and preparation for ministerial training

i) We believe that theological education should be available widely, for lay and ordained alike. However, the current provision for formal lay theological education in the dioceses is uneven and rarely draws on the combined resources of the dioceses and the training institutions. We recommend a new initiative in this area under the general title of 'Education for Discipleship'.

ii) Candidates coming forward for training today show a great variety of prior learning. Some have significant appropriate learning but, in general, many are less securely grounded in a knowledge of the Scriptures and the Church's tradition than in previous generations. As a result we believe that potential ordinands should be encouraged to undertake a significant level of theological study and ministerial exploration (for example, 60–120 credit points at Level 1 in higher education terms)[2] before formally starting training. Candidates who have undertaken such preliminary studies should have a much better idea of the nature of the study of theology and have begun an exploration of the range of possible ministries.

iv) Programmes of learning that would be of interest both to lay people in general and to potential ministerial candidates could also offer much to training programmes for Readers, lay pastoral assistants and other lay ministries.

---

[2] In brief, Level 1 equates to year one of full-time study in higher education. It can be taken in a part-time mode in, for example, two years. Put in terms of credit points, Level 1 is 120 credit points, while 60 credit points is half of Level 1, approximately equivalent to one year of part-time study.

Proposal 3

We recommend that

i) opportunities for learning, under the general title of Education for Discipleship, are offered on a Church-wide basis for a range of students, which might include lay people seeking to deepen their Christian discipleship, trainee Readers and other lay ministers and potential candidates for ordination;

ii) prospective ordinands are encouraged to engage in such preliminary studies before they enter training;

iii) for prospective ordinands the amount and level of such studies should be decided in the light of the candidate's abilities, needs and circumstances, with the guideline that candidates with no prior formal learning in theology for ministry are encouraged to attain 60–120 credit points at Level 1, or its equivalent.

8 Norms for the qualification for the clergy

While the clergy are primarily disciples of Jesus Christ and ministers of the Church, they are also leaders of communities and need to minister in a professional manner. We note the rising expectations of the clergy, the increased accreditation of vocational training generally and that other professions, such as nursing and teaching, are increasingly graduate professions. As a result, we would suggest, stated generally and as a norm, that clergy who exercise an oversight ministry (for example as an incumbent or senior chaplain) should achieve graduate level in ministerial theology and practice. In more detail, we propose that, as a norm, all candidates should achieve diploma level by the time of ordination and that those who are to be appointed to a post of responsibility would be expected to reach degree level in ministerial theology and practice by the time of their appointment. OLMs and those stipendiary and non-stipendiary clergy who will minister in an assistant capacity should continue with their learning in the first years of ministry with a view to being equipped for the envisaged ministry. Of course many clergy will have already achieved the norm of degree level in ministerial theology and practice by the time of ordination. They would be expected to continue their learning and ministerial development through an appropriate postgraduate vocational qualification or other accredited or non-accredited learning.

Proposal 4: We recommend, as a series of norms, that:

i) **candidates for ordained ministry should have successfully achieved a minimum of diploma level in ministerial theology and practice before ordination;**

ii) **they continue with further learning at an agreed level according to their ability in the post-ordination phase of IME;**

iii) **typically, those who are to hold posts of responsibility (for example, team vicars, some chaplains or incumbents) achieve a minimum of degree level in ministerial theology and practice, or its equivalent, by the time of appointment to a post of responsibility.**

9 Towards new institutional arrangements for training

i) The Church of England has a good track record in the creation of a variety of types of ministerial and lay education. Its resources in this area include:

- theological colleges, regional courses and OLM schemes that offer training and formation for ordained ministry;

- diocesan provision for training for Reader ministry, of other lay ministries and for lay discipleship and CME for clergy and Readers;

- ecumenical partnerships in training;

- partnership with UK higher education, with both the universities and the Church colleges of higher education.

However, when looked at as a whole, the Church's training resources are dispersed in a large number of mainly very small institutions or units, which are not related to each other in a systematic way. Thus, for example, for around 1400 ordination candidates the Church makes use of twelve theological colleges (including one in Wales), twelve regional courses and 19 OLM schemes, a total of 43 small institutions. To this must be added 44 units that provide Reader training, CME and other programmes in individual dioceses. While this situation has come about through complex historical development, it has resulted in a training provision that does not now fully reflect the Church's needs for the coming decades. Rather than training institutions being organized for discrete groups of students, as in the past, our current and future needs are for institutes that can train candidates for particular ministries while enabling lay and ordained to grow and learn together for the corporate tasks of mission and ministry.

ii) While the small size of these institutions has some real benefits, it also has a range of adverse effects in most settings. These include

- small staffs, with a necessarily limited range of subject and ministerial expertise;

- the contribution of our training institutions to the life of the Church in terms of research, enabling the Church to think clearly and deeply about issues arising from the faith or from the Church's mission, is very limited, because staff energies are focused on the immediate tasks of training and of running the institutions;

- the smallness of institutions means that the burden of Church and university supervisory and quality control procedures is disproportionate to the size of the institution.

iii) Our training institutions are not currently set up to deliver ministerial education from entry into training to the end of the first curacy as envisaged in Proposal 1. Ministerial education is currently delivered by colleges, courses and OLM schemes on the one hand, and by training incumbents and diocesan provision for CME on the other.

iv) While all colleges and courses and some dioceses have entered into some form of partnership with UK higher education, each small unit has done so either on its own or in clusters. This is very time-consuming, and raises the wider question whether the Church is maximizing the potential of this partnership. This is the case both with regard to entering these partnerships on equal terms, leading to mature and mutually beneficial arrangements, and in terms of the Church's contribution to the study of Christian theology within institutions of higher education as a witness to the faith.

v) As a result of these factors, and in order to resource the mission of the Church through the provision of better training for clergy and lay alike, we believe that there is a strong case for reconfiguring our training provision. Despite its many achievements, the current provision of colleges, courses, OLM schemes and diocesan training units cannot, for structural reasons, deliver the integrated and coherent IME which we believe is necessary. Thus, in the light of our analysis as a working party, we do not believe that the status quo is an option that we can recommend.

vi) However, any successful plan for the future will need to harness in a positive way the considerable financial, staffing and training resources of our whole training establishment – diocesan, college, course and OLM schemes, with their potential for creative partnership with higher education in the United Kingdom. Further, while some current ministerial training is ecumenical in character, this review gives the opportunity to enter into a new phase of ecumenical partnership.

As a result of these reflections we envisage new training partnerships in which the dioceses, other churches and our existing training provision would be the stakeholders.

Proposal 5

We recommend the creation of new institutional arrangements for training through structured and effective partnerships, drawing on diocesan training establishments (including OLM schemes), theological colleges and courses, in collaboration both with other churches and with UK higher education. The purposes of the new training partnerships should be:

i) to provide initial ministerial education for the clergy from entry into training to the end of the first training post;

ii) to develop expertise in particular areas of mission and ministry to enhance training for ordination and other ministries and types of service;

iii) to contribute to the initial training of Readers and other lay ministers and to continuing ministerial education for all ministries;

iv) to contribute to the formal theological education of the laity through the provision of programmes of Education for Discipleship;

v) to provide capacity to do research for the benefit of the Church.

10 A regional model for training partnerships

Our starting point for considering models for new institutional arrangements was the Church of England's total resources in the area of training for ministry and for lay discipleship. Having reviewed the options we believe that a regional model, based on about eight regions, would best serve the needs of the Church. These could provide strong partnerships that remain in a dynamic relationship with the localities they serve. It is vital that local initiatives continue to revitalize theological education. With regard to ordination training, we would invite the dioceses and other churches, with the existing colleges, courses and OLM schemes, to enter into these partnerships. In turn, we would envisage that it would be these partnerships that would be recognized for ordination training by the House of Bishops. The resources of the partnerships could also provide high-quality CME, Reader training and programmes under the Education for Discipleship initiative. With regard to the number and boundaries of the proposed regions, we believe that this should be decided in full consultation with the affected parties in a separate exercise once the Church has decided in principle to go down this route. In the full report we provide some possible illustrations of an eight-region approach.

Proposal 6

We recommend:

i) **the creation of regional theological training partnerships, with each partnership offering the range of training and education listed in Proposal 5;**

ii) **that the House of Bishops grants its recognition for ordination training to these regional training partnerships.**

11 Financial issues

As a working party we think it right for the Church to invest significantly in high-quality and cost-effective training for the clergy and for other forms of ministry and discipleship. Further, we believe that the scope for significant overall savings is limited but that the Church could get a higher quality and more extensive training for its investment. We have looked at a series of financial issues:

- the main drivers of the costs of ordination training in its various forms;

- whether there is a way of redirecting the balance of expenditure from personal and family maintenance (currently 46 per cent of the total expenditure on ordination training) to education and training;

- whether there is a way of increasing the contribution of public funding to ordination training;

- the need to develop a funding framework that gives some stability to our training institutions, to allow them to plan, and which controls costs in the light of the type of candidate coming forward for the various forms of ministry;

- a funding formula for the research dimension of proposed new institutions.

12 The financial benefits of partnership

While there are intrinsic benefits in our proposal for structured and effective partnerships between the current separate training units, we also believe that there are net savings to be gained through partnership. While there will be some modest start-up costs, we assume that a saving of 7.5 per cent can be made in the two areas of administrative and academic costs. At the same time there is a need for the new partnerships to cooperate in order to get the maximum benefit from IT.

Proposal 7

We recommend that regional training partnerships:

i) **share administrative services and academic staff with a view to making savings.**

ii) **work closely together to maximize the benefits obtained from the appropriate use of Information and**

Communication Technology for learning and for formation.

13 Public funding for ministerial training?

We have investigated in some detail the possibility of additional direct or indirect public funding for ministerial training, through setting training for ordination within higher education institutions funded by the Higher Education Funding Council for England (HEFCE). This is a complex area and not one without risk for the Church. However, there may be possible benefit to be gained and therefore we make a cautious recommendation.

Proposal 8

We recommend that the Ministry Division and the proposed regional partnerships should investigate further and evaluate the possibility of benefiting from HEFCE funding.

14 Three-year funding base

As we noted above, it is important both for training institutions to have some stability in order to plan for the future and for the Church to be able to respond to changes in the number and type of ordinands and other candidates for ministry coming forward. As a result we propose a bidding process for funding that has a three-year rolling base.

Proposal 9

We recommend that the regional training partnerships bid for funds on a three-year rolling basis from the Ministry Division.

15 Funding our proposals

15.1 We are recommending a new shape for ministerial education in the future through our proposals to extend IME into the early years of ministry and to deliver this training through structured and effective institutional partnership on a regional basis. This in turn will mean a new relationship between the dioceses and the training institutions, which will need to be reflected in staffing and financial matters. Our proposals here are that dioceses, as well as ministerial training institutions, should be active partners in the proposed RTPs. They should continue to provide CME officers and Adult Education officers but, for this aspect of their work, they should commit the relevant staff to the regional partnership. By working in this way, the funding of CME and Adult Education officers will continue to be a diocesan matter and not a cost that is shared through the General Synod budget (known as Vote 1) and apportionment.

15.2 With regard to the funding of the post-ordination phase of IME, we believe that this additional cost should be funded by a reduction of 75 in the number of full-time candidates requiring family support in theological colleges. The savings made from this future transfer of candidates to part-time modes of training should be used to fund our proposals for strengthening training in the first years of ministry and for research.

Proposal 10

We recommend that:

i) **diocesan officers for OLM training, for the post-ordination phase of IME of the clergy, for Reader and other lay theological education including Education for Discipleship should continue to be provided by their own dioceses but are committed by their dioceses to work within the regional partnership for the relevant aspects of their work;**

ii) savings initially in the region of £1,000,000 per annum should be made within Vote 1 by a reduction of about 75 in the number of people requiring family support who train on a full-time basis and that this saving be used to fund additional costs of CME 1–4, being £700,000 for accredited training and £300,000 for residence or equivalent training.

16 Research and its funding

We have noted above the need for a research capacity in our training institutions. This is a priority for two main reasons. Firstly, high-quality teaching can only be achieved if staff are up-to-date and contributing to their field of expertise. Secondly, the Church needs good-quality research in theology and in the practice of mission and ministry in order to inform its life and witness. In the light of this we propose that research is funded at a level equivalent to one post in each of the proposed eight RTPs and that this sum be found out of savings proposed elsewhere in this report. In practice we would expect this funding to be significantly enhanced by partnership arrangements with other interested parties and by institutions seeking their own funding base for research.

Proposal 11

We recommend that budgetary provision initially in the region of £240,000 in total per annum should be made within Vote 1 to fund research within each regional training partnership.

17 The scope of Vote 1

At the present, funding for ordination training is divided between:

i) central Church funding for fees, i.e. tuition costs and, for candidates in colleges, term-time maintenance of the candidate in college. This money is approved each year in the General Synod Vote 1 budget, the cost of which is then shared between the dioceses according to the apportionment formula.

ii) family maintenance and vacation support of single students, which is initially paid by the sponsoring diocese and is then shared across the dioceses through a pooling arrangement.

By both these mechanisms, the cost of training for ordination is spread between the dioceses. We make a cost-neutral proposal that family and single maintenance (ii above) continues to be scrutinized and administered at diocesan level, but the payments should be made centrally as part of the Vote 1 budget. This will enable the budgeted savings on family maintenance costs suggested in Proposal 10 ii to be re-allocated to fund the proposed increase in expenditure on training and formation. Equally, the proposed expenditure on research (Proposal 11) should be included within the scope of Vote 1.

Proposal 12

We recommend that the scope of Vote 1 should be expanded to cover all central costs of initial ministerial education as defined in Proposal 1, including personal and family maintenance for married and single candidates and research.

18 The Three-year Rolling Reserve

As recommended in the report Managing Planned Growth (GS Misc 597, January 2000), if in any year the expenditure on Vote 1 is less than budget, the saving is held in a Three-year Rolling Reserve so as to meet any overspends in subsequent years if there is a sharp increase in the number of candidates in training. We believe that this is a valuable mechanism and would propose that it be retained.

Proposal 13

We recommend that the Three-year Rolling Reserve mechanism be retained and that, subject to approval by Synod, any available balance may be used, as now, to smooth the impact on Vote 1 of any approved increase in the funding required as a result of an increase in the number of sponsored candidates.

19 Financial outlook

In order to produce a financial forecast for the cost of ordination training in the coming years we have made the following assumptions:

i) there is no change in the number of candidates being ordained;

ii) our proposals are implemented in full by 2008;

iii) at the same time, as part of its normal work, the Ministry Division will reduce the base on which core costs for college training are calculated by 50 in order to reflect the current decline in the numbers in college-type training;

On these assumptions, we estimate that a saving in the region of £500,000 per annum will arise. The projected savings over the next six years are set out below:

Year	Total Vote 1 for existing establishment £	Reduce core costs by 50 places £	Effect of our proposals £	Total reduction in costs £	Revised total Vote 1 £
2003	12,181,504	-52,946	0	-52,946	12,128,558
2004	12,493,053	-218,680	-120,342	-339,022	12,154,031
2005	12,884,288	-336,561	-540,734	-877,294	12,006,994
2006	13,310,949	-342,899	-621,667	-964,566	12,346,383
2007	13,740,908	-356,615	-273,471	-630,086	13,110,822
2008	14,163,791	-369,810	-128,234	-498,043	13,665,748

20 Encouraging and managing flexibility in pathways through training

i) Our proposals for the extension of IME to the end of the first training post and for the creation of regional training partnerships will offer an important opportunity to devise new pathways through training for candidates. As at present, some candidates will move to college-type training outside of their own region, while others will train within the region. Within each region there will be the opportunity for full-time and various part-time modes of training, and for the creation of new patterns of training combining these modes. We would encourage the development of new and creative patterns of training, making full use of the period from entry into training through to the end of the first training post.

ii) Currently the content, level and balance of training programmes are scrutinized and approved by the Ministry

Division's Educational Validation Panel. In order to ensure common standards of training across the Church this work should continue and be extended to include the post-ordination phase of IME.

iii) With regard to training plans for candidates, we have proposed above that there should be greater flexibility about choices of part-time and full-time modes of training, or combinations of these modes. Our proposals will enable dioceses and trainers to construct individual training plans for particular candidates where the need arises.

iv) With regard to the choice of whether a candidate trains in a college or in a part-time mode, or in a combination of types, we propose that the sponsoring diocese initiates the discussion about an individual candidate. Final agreement should be reached between the sponsoring bishop, advised by the DDO, and the relevant RTP, drawing on the advice of the Ministry Division as necessary. As with standard programmes of training, it will be valuable for the educational and formation content of individual training plans to be approved at a national level in order to maintain common standards in training.

Proposal 14

We recommend that:

i) **flexible pathways through training are developed, drawing on college, course and OLM types of training and other resources, in order to meet the training needs of candidates;**

ii) **the current approach to validating routes for ordinands on standard programmes be continued and be extended to the pre- and post-ordination phases of IME as defined in this report;**

iii) the sponsoring diocese initiates the discussion about the appropriate pathway through training for individual candidates and that the final decision is made through agreement between the sponsoring bishop, advised by the DDO, and the relevant regional training partnership;

iv) an appropriate procedure be devised for the Ministry Division to scrutinize and approve the individual training plans of candidates training on non-standard programmes, and to give advice on the training of candidates not agreed under iii) above.

21 Implementation

It has been our task as a working party to think through the basic issues and to make proposals that can guide the Church in the next phase of the development of ministerial training and theological education. If these proposals are adopted there will be a further substantial task, for the Church of England and its ecumenical partners, to implement these proposals appropriately in a range of different local settings. This will require implementation arrangements to be made at national and regional levels.

Proposal 15

We recommend that appropriate arrangements be made for the implementation of this report at the national and regional levels.

22 Ecumenical implications

The working party has benefited from representation from the Methodist and United Reformed Church on it and has kept other partners in initial training fully informed of its progress, both directly and through the Ecumenical Strategy Group for Ministerial Training. We see our proposals as an opportunity for renewed ecumenical partnership in ministerial training and theological education. As such, it will be vital for the report to be implemented with full ecumenical participation.

23 Outlook

In line with our terms of reference, we have undertaken a wide-ranging review of the initial training needs of the clergy in the light of the Church's mission. This has led us to make a range of proposals to strengthen the formation and education offered to ministers, lay and ordained, and to reconfigure the Church's training resources to support those aims. We are under no illusions about the size and complexity of the task if our proposals were to be accepted and implemented. This will require a great deal of vision, charity, hard work and persistence – in fact, the courage to cease working in familiar ways and to think through and implement new ways, in order to serve the Church's mission. At the same time, having tested our proposals through debate and consultation, we believe that they offer the Church – and the society it seeks to serve – a platform for the dynamic development of ministerial training and lay education in the coming decades.

Appendix A
Terms of reference and membership of the working party on the structure and funding of ordination training

A. Terms of reference

i) Building on the work of the Vote 1 review group, to consider and advise on the wider issues identified in that report concerning the funding and structure of initial training for ordination.

ii) To review the training needs of the Church in the light of developing patterns of ministry and the Church's future needs in ministry.

iii) To comment on the specific areas listed by the Vote 1 report:

- Diversification by colleges and courses – wider issues

- Exploring the different types and length of training

- Funding of research in colleges and courses

- Impact of lay ministry and other authorized ministries on the number of stipendiary clergy needed

- Incorporation of pooling costs within the apportionment

- Possible economies of scale through fewer institutions

- Sponsorship category for ordained ministry (stipendiary and non-stipendiary)

- Ways of working with the wider church to reduce overheads.

B. Membership – follows on the next page

Membership of the working party on structure and funding of ordination training

Chairman	The Rt Revd John Hind	Bishop of Gibraltar in Europe; now Bishop of Chichester
Member of the House of Bishops	The Rt Revd Dr Peter Forster	Bishop of Chester
Ministry expertise	The Revd Canon Keith Lamdin	Director of the Board of Stewardship, Training, Evangelism and Ministry – Diocese of Oxford
	The Revd Canon June Osborne	Treasurer, Salisbury Cathedral; Bishops' Inspector
	The Revd Canon Dr Robin Greenwood	Ministry Development Officer – Diocese of Chelmsford; now, as an Observer, Provincial Officer for Ministry, Church in Wales
Training expertise	The Revd Dr Richard Burridge	Dean, King's College, London; Member of Vote 1 Working Party; member of General Synod
	The Revd Dr Judith Maltby	Chaplain – Corpus Christi College, Oxford
Finance expertise	The Revd Barry Nichols (Vice Chairman)	Chairman – Vote 1 Working Party
		Retired partner – Ernst & Young
	Mr Richard Finlinson	Chairman – Canterbury DBF
Training institutions	The Revd Dr Jeremy Sheehy	Principal, St Stephen's House, Oxford
	The Revd Canon Dr David Hewlett	Principal, South West Ministry Training Course; Director of the Queen's Foundation, Birmingham from April 2003
	The Revd Canon Wendy Bracegirdle	Principal, Manchester OLM Scheme (until December 2002)
Diocesan	Mr Phil Hamlyn-Williams	Reader; Lincoln Diocesan Secretary; Member of Vote 1 Working Party; Member of Archbishops' Finance Committee
	Mr Anthony Archer	St Albans Diocese; member of General Synod
Church Colleges of Higher Education	Professor Dianne Willcocks	Principal of York St John College, formerly the College of Ripon and York St John
Ecumenical members	The Revd Don Pickard	Formation in Ministry Office, Methodist Church
	The Revd Roy Lowes (from February 2002)	Secretary for Training, United Reformed Church
Assessors	Mr Richard Hopgood (until July 2002)	Archbishops' Council: Director of Policy
	The Ven Dr Gordon Kuhrt	Director of Ministry
Secretaries	Mr David Morris	Archbishops' Council Ministry Division: Finance & Administrative Secretary
	The Revd Dr David Way	Theological Education Secretary
	Miss Sarah Evans	Secretariat

www.ingramcontent.com/pod-product-compliance
Lightning Source LLC
Chambersburg PA
CBHW072116290426
44110CB00014B/1937